The Devil in the White City

: A Saga of Magic and Murder at the Fair that Changed America

by Erik Larson

: This is a quick read summary based on the book "The Devil in the White City" by Erik Larson

Note to Readers:

This is a Summary & Analysis of "The Devil in the White City" by Erik Larson. You are encouraged to buy the full version.

TABLE OF CONTENTS

OVERVIEW

The Devil in the White City: Murder, Magic, and Madness at the Fair that Changed America by Erik Larson, published in 2002, is an historical work centered on the Chicago World's Fair of 1893. More specifically, the focus of the author centers on two men and their accomplishments during this pivotal moment in the history of America's new modern era. The first is the chief architect of the fair, Daniel Burnham, whose vision shaped the fair, and by extension, the architectural aesthetic of modern cities more broadly speaking for the generations that followed. His story is one of the power of creation fueled by persistence in the face of obstacles. The second focus of the book is America's first known serial killer, Dr. H. H. Holmes, whose acts of evil during the time of the World's Fair would manifest a destructive power that lived in the shadows of metropolitan anonymity.

This review offers a detailed summary of the main themes raised in this historical work. In general the summary follows the structure of the book, which is largely presented in chronological order, alternating between the main historical figures central to the story. However, parts of the summary are presented in an order that deviates slightly from that of the book in order to preserve the continuity and readability of the facts presented. The summary is followed by an analysis.

Larson is both an accomplished journalist and historical novelist. He has written four *New York Times* bestselling books. He has written for *The Wall Street Journal* and *Time Magazine* as a staff journalist. He has been a contributing author to *The Atlantic, Harper's,* and *The New Yorker.* His academic background includes a bachelors in Russian history, language and culture from the University of Pennsylvania, and a Masters in journalism from Columbia University.

SUMMARY

PROLOGUE: ABOARD THE OLYMPIC, 1912

In this brief opening section of the book, Larson explains how on April 12, 1912, one of the only surviving architects of the 1893 Chicago World's Fair was on board a ship called the *R.M.S. Olympic*, owned by the White Star Line. His name was Daniel Hudson Burnham, and he was the chief builder of the fair. Simultaneously, and traveling in the other direction on the *Olympic's* sister ship, was another of the three architects still living, Francis Millet. Millet and Burnham remained close friends. Upon trying to send him a telegram, however, he discovered that the ship Millet was on had an accident and that the *Olympic* had changed course to intercept and offer aid.

Much of the rest of this introduction is devoted to giving the reader a sense of scale for this great and wondrous world's fair.

Despite a mountain of administrative and regulatory hurdles, the fair opened and received 27.5 million visitors over the course of six months during a time when the population of America was only 65 million people. The fair was wildly held as a modern marvel and it was significant in shifting the national imagination concerning technology and architecture. New foods such as Cracker Jacks and Shredded Wheat were on offer. The grand exhibit hall was a monumental feat of architecture for the time and had enough interior volume to have contained St. Paul's Cathedral, Madison Square Garden, the Great Pyramid, the U.S. Capital building and Winchester Cathedral, combined. In addition to the great achievement of the fair, it also came at a human cost of workers that died during the construction, a great fire, an assassination, and the victims of America's first known serial killer. The story contained is largely that of two exceptional men: one known for his great capacity for creation, the other for his great capacity for destruction, both active during this pivotal historical event at the dawn of modern America.

PART I: FROZEN MUSIC, CHICAGO, 1890-91

The city of Chicago in 1890 was a place of great social transformation as turn of the century urban life was taking shape. One feature of metropolitan living was the anonymity that was created by a thousand trains a day bringing in people from all over the country looking for a new life. Many among them were young single women looking for office or garment industry work. The city had bars, houses of prostitution, and gambling establishments. Social commentators of the time considered the persistence of these vices in the city, a regular subject of debate in the press. Chicago had a particularly bad reputation at the time for being associated with organized crime. There were also many dangers such as people being maimed and killed by trains, streetcars, carriages and fires. Infectious disease took many lives as well. In addition, murder was common by today's standards with almost 800 homicides in the first six months of 1892. Police forces were generally undermanned to the task of properly handling this high volume of crime.

The city had recently been counted as the second most populous city in the nation at just over a million, beating out Philadelphia which had previously held the title. On February 24, 1890 people gathered across the city to await an announcement concerning whether or not the city would host the World's Fair. The smoke in the streets on that cold day reduced visibility considerably. Daniel Burnham who was 43 years old, and his 40 year old partner, John Root, also awaited the announcement from their office on the top floor of the Rookery. Considered the leading architects of the city, the two had become known for their work across the country constructing the first skyscrapers, each larger than the next. They had already participated in behind the scenes conversations with top officials concerning the fair, but on this day they too waited for the official announcement.

The original idea for the fair was a celebration of the 400 year anniversary of Columbus's discovery of the continent. However, the idea did not gather much steam until 1889 when France astounded the world with the Exposition Universelle, the highlight of which was the new Eiffel Tower, the highest manmade structure on earth at the time. The poor showing of the American displays in contrast to those of the French at that event ignited a passion for many Americans who did not want to be outdone by the French.

The site for the fair was a matter of some controversy. Among the serious contenders were Washington D.C., St. Louis, and of course New York. Chicago's claim rested largely on the pride of having rebuilt the city to a new splendor and in short order after the Great Fire of 1871. There was a great amount of rivalry between Chicago and New York at the time, and those in Chicago were anxious to put to rest any notion that their city was second to New York. The final decision was left to a congressional vote.

The news came to the *Chicago Tribune* by a telegraph from Washington and updates to the count were posted in the window of the *Tribune* offices. The publishers prepared a special "extra" edition for the final count with newspaper boys on standby to spread the news throughout the city. The initial count came in just after four o'clock and showed Chicago was first followed by New York (trailing by 43 votes), St. Louis then Washington, although no city had the clear majority needed to outright win the fair so the voting continued. The crowds broke into shouts of jubilations. By the fifth report, which came in at dusk to a growing crowd, the gap had thinned and the crowd began to have a palpable gloominess. The crowd remained despite the announcement of a brief adjournment lobbied for by the New York cadre of congressmen. Suspense was thick across town at the seventh ballot, when it was announced that Chicago was only a single vote shy of the necessary majority.

The author then shifts his attention to Daniel Hudson Burnham. He was born on September 4, 1846 in the town of Henderson, New York. His family practiced Swedenborgianism, a Christian sect that valued self-subordination, obedience and service to others. The family moved to Chicago when Burnham was nine years old where his father was a successful druggist. Burnham was a mediocre student who excelled with drawing, and his father was able to send him to study with private tutors to help him prepare for the entrance exams to Yale and Harvard, but severe test anxiety proved to undo him and he was declined admission to both schools which would impact him deeply and permanently.

He returned to Chicago and found a draftsman position at Loring & Jenney, an architectural firm and immediately took to the work and realized his calling to be an architect. A year later he joined some friends in a gold mining venture that failed in Nevada, followed by another failure at a seat in the Nevada legislature. Broke, he returned to Chicago and worked for another architectural firm, L. G. Laurean. In October of 1871 the Great Fire wiped out 18,000 buildings leaving over 100,000 people without homes. At a time when the architects of the city had endless work, Burnham quit the firm and failed at two more ventures: selling plate glass and working as a druggist.

At twenty-five years old he joined the firm of Peter Wight, at his father's request. It was here that he first met John Wellborn Root who was also drafting at the firm. Root was born January 10, 1850 in Lumpkin, Georgia. He was a musical prodigy and his father sent him to England during the Civil War. He was accepted to Oxford, but the war ended and he moved to New York City before graduating. He majored in civil engineering at New York University. The two soon became partners and had their first job as a firm in 1873. The partnership kept Burnham engaged despite difficult economic times following the 1873 market crash. In 1874, John B. Sherman, superintendent of the Union Stock Yards, commissioned the partners to build his personal mansion among the homes of other titans of industry on Prairie Avenue and Twenty-First Street. The Union Sock Yards was a huge operation employing over 25,000 people and which slaughtered over 14 million animals annually. That the city was known for its meatpacking industry did not help its reputation among the cultural elites of other large cities of the day.

During the project Burnham became engaged to John Sherman's daughter Margaret and the couple married in January of 1876. Sherman wanted the couple close to him as he had some concerns about Burnham's drinking and so he bought them a home at Forty-Third Street and Michigan Avenue, not far from the stockyards. However, his respect for Burnham's work did not wane and he commissioned several other structures from the firm including granting them the honor of building the entrance to the great stockyards. The enormous gate was constructed of Lemont limestone with copper roofing and featured a carved statue of Sherman's favorite bull (named Sherman). Root married Mary Walker, daughter of the president of the Union Stock Yards, John Walker. During their engagement she developed tuberculosis but Root remained committed. Within six weeks of the marriage Mary died. He married again two years later, this time to Dora Monroe, whose sister would later write Root's biography, and by all accounts was likely in love with him.

The geological terrain of Chicago had presented architects with significant hurdles for building large structures. There was bedrock, but it was 125 feet below the surface which eluded the contemporary building technology. The ground above the bedrock was a mix of clay and sand that compressed under the weight of large structures and was an unwieldy foundation for large buildings. The only solution so far included drilling caissons that had to be pressurized with air to keep water from seeping in while workers constructed pylons to anchor into the bedrock below. This technique, developed for bridge building, had notoriously killed an alarming rate of 20 percent of those that entered the caissons due to the bends, a condition caused by pressurized environments. However, the rapidly rising real estate costs of downtown Chicago created an ever increasing demand to solve this technical problem.

The partners were commissioned by Peter Chardon Brooks III to build the tallest structure at the time in Chicago, the

Montauk. The traditional solution to the problem of large buildings was to build pyramids of stone upon which columns would bear the load of the building that would distribute the weight more evenly, reducing the settling effect of the unstable ground below. However, it limited the size of the buildings since larger buildings required larger pyramids to support their weight. If this method were used for a building the size of the Montauk, there would be no basement left for the dynamo and boilers needed to generate the electricity and heat for the building. This created a dilemma that Root was determined to solve.

The solution that came to Root was deceptively simple. Workers would carve down to the layer of hardpan clay and lay a "floating foundation" constructed of poured cement and alternating layers of steel beams that spanned the length of the foundation, each layer at right angles to the next. This solution worked and the Montauk became the first true skyscraper ever built. Combined with innovations in steel load bearing frames developed by William Jenney, the final constraints to height were lifted and the heyday of skyscraper construction was underway.

Burnham and Root became quite wealthy as a result of their participation in the skyscraper boom. The partnership brought out the best in the complimentary talents of both men. Roots was more skilled with the design end of the business, Burnham in sales and execution. Burnham, whose charisma derived from stunning good looks and a confident demeanor, recognized that Root was the more artistically gifted of the pair. The city grew alongside the firm, both taller and grander as well as dirtier and more dangerous. Smoke from coal fueled dynamos and furnaces created a smog that reduced visibility, sometimes to less than a block. The sounds of all of the various transportation systems created an ongoing deafening roar to the streets that did not abate until after midnight. Poorly funded city maintenance crews meant that streets, particularly in poor neighborhoods, were piled with trash and the corpses of animals, along with the ensuing scourges of flies. The effect of Chicago on visitors was both awe and horror.

In 1886, now the father of five children, Burnham shared these mixed views of Chicago and bought some country land with a large farmhouse in the small town of Evanston. Although the firm was successful, it was not without challenges. One in particular was the collapse during construction of a Kansas City hotel the firm was building. The inquest over the accident was public, and stressful. Another blow came when the city, deciding to focus on an architectural achievement showcasing culture (in response to the claims from rival New York that Chicago lacked culture), made a decision to build a giant auditorium. Although most assumed the contract would go to Burnham & Root, it was instead awarded to Dankmar Adler on account of his demonstrated skills with mastering acoustics. This would initiate a rivalry with the Adler and his partner Louis Sullivan that would span decades.

At this point the author returns to the scene of the crowd waiting outside of the *Chicago Tribune* awaiting the final vote on which city the World's Fair would be awarded to. When the news broke that it was going to be awarded to Chicago, the crowd burst into screams and messenger boys raced off in every direction. A corporation was immediately founded in Chicago, called the World's Columbian Exposition Company, to finance and oversee the construction and operations of the fair. It was quietly announced that Burnham and Root would be the chief architects of the endeavor. The pressure was extraordinary since it involved transforming essentially an entire city in three years. In addition, it needed to significantly rival the French or it would be perceived as a great failure which would deal a devastating blow to the firm. It also needed to be profitable.

The author turns here to the arrival of H. H. Holmes at a train station in Chicago in August of 1886. He was handsome and charismatic, with his most striking feature being large blue eyes that laid upon others longer than was conventionally polite, a habit that women apparently found very captivating. He arrived in Englewood, a town south of Chicago near the Union Stock Yards. He walked until he came upon Holton Drugs, on the corner of Wallace and Sixty-third. Across the street was a vacant lot. He went in and introduced himself to the proprietor, Mrs. Holton, as a doctor and pharmacist. It turned out that her husband was dying and he offered his help to handle the business of the store and turn it into a thriving business. After consulting with her husband, she accepted his offer.

His given name was actually Herman Webster Mudgett. He grew up in the very small town of Gilmanton Academy where he was the subject of derision among other young children. He had a brother and a sister. His father, like his grandfather, was a farmer. The family was Methodist with strict sanctions for misbehavior including corporal punishment, enforced prayer, and seclusion to the attic with no food. He enjoyed reading Jules Verne and Edgar Allen Poe and he also enjoyed building things.

He had a solitary close friend as a child who died from a fall when the boys were playing in an old house. When he was sixteen he graduated and became a teacher. He moved to Alton, New Hampshire and met a woman named Clara A.

Lovering. They married when he was eighteen on July 4, 1878. The initial high passion of the marriage quickly turned cold and Mudget spent increasingly long periods away from the house until he disappeared entirely. Despite their separation, the two remained legally married.

Mudgett attended medical school at nineteen, first at University of Vermont, then University of Michigan in Ann Arbor. He matriculated in 1884 with mediocre performance. He then traveled on some business for a nursery to scout for a good location, settling on Mooers Forks, New York where he was hired as a school principle until he could establish his medical practice. While he lived in that town a young boy he had been seen with had gone missing. However, townsfolk accepted his explanation that he had sent the boy home to Massachusetts with no further investigation.

His financial situation, however, was not strong. He and a former classmate hatched a plan to commit insurance fraud, a plan which is described in some detail in the memoir written by Homes while awaiting trial. The plan centered on finding three cadavers in an advanced state of decomposition which would pass as the dead bodies of a family, played by other accomplices, who were insured with one of the other accomplices as a beneficiary. They decided to divide the task of acquiring bodies. Doctors in that era of medicine routinely used cadavers for dissection and experimentation. Mudgett claims to have acquired the bodies he was responsible for in Chicago on an 1885 trip, but unable to acquire a job in the city, he put them in storage and returned to Minneapolis where he worked in a drug store until 1886. He then went to New York City with part of the body in tow. He claims that he was turned away from the idea of executing the plan on the train ride to New York when he read a story about the insurance companies increasing vigilance on such fraud, although the author maintains this is a fabrication.

The author argues that even the statement of financial need is unlikely given that the owner of the lodging where Mudgett stayed during his time at Mooers Fork stated that he was often seen with cash. He left Mooers Fork in the middle of the night and headed for Philadelphia where he took a job at the Norristown Asylum but then left three days later claiming that it was too disturbing. He found a job at a drugstore in Philadelphia, and then left soon afterwards when a child died from medicine purchased at the store. He left for Chicago, but discovered he could not practice as a druggist until he passed a state licensure exam, so at that time he borrowed the name Holmes, a prominent family name of that generation.

After Holmes worked at the drugstore in Englewood for a short time, Dr. Holton died. He offered to buy the store from Mrs. Holton in an arrangement where she could continue to live in the apartment upstairs which she graciously accepted. The purchase was financed by putting a lien on the merchandise in the store itself. He soon renamed the establishment: H. H. Holmes Pharmacy, and once word spread that a single and young doctor operated the business, single women flocked to the establishment. Established clientele inquired as to the whereabouts of Mrs. Holton, who

Holmes claimed was on an extended visit with family out west, later claiming that she had moved there.

The author returns to the planning of the fair and notes that six months after the decision the board of directors, consisting of forty-five prominent men of the city, had failed to agree even on a location for the event. The stalemate based on territorial politicking was frustrating to both Burnham as well as other members of the board, one of whom was James Ellsworth. Ellsworth hired prominent designer of Central Park, Fredrick Law Olmsted, with his own money to come and assess Chicago and offer sound consulting advice to try to sway the board to a decision. Olmsted agreed somewhat reluctantly.

Olmsted and the newest member of his firm, Henry Sargent Codman, arrived in Chicago in August of 1890. Burnham and Root were partial to a location named Jackson Park which was located south of Chicago on the lakeshore near Englewood. As it turns out, Olmsted had studied the area in depth some years before for a park in the area commissioned by the city, plans for which were scrapped because of the Great Fire. He agreed on the location, despite being aware of some potential building issues, and wrote a report to that effect to the board of directors. Included in the report was a lecture on the importance of working together for a project of this undertaking to succeed. He also articulated a vision whereby each element of the fair should evoke in some small way the larger vision of the great spectacle. He highlighted the importance of the proximity of the Lake as a critical natural feature, the only of Chicago, which would add immeasurably to the grandeur required of the event. Despite a strongly worded letter expressing his preferences and urging the board to act quickly, the decision on location was still not made by the end of October 1890.

At this juncture, the author makes a quick detour to introduce the reader to Patrick Eugene Joseph Prendergast, a twenty-two year old who ran a crew of newsboys for the *Chicago Inter Ocean*. Prendergast was an Irish immigrant whose family immigrated just in time to experience the Great Fire. He was a very quiet and shy child but became interested in politics, notably the Single-Tax movement which advocated a property tax. He was also an avid supporter of former mayor Carter Henry Harrison and wrote many postcards to prominent men of the city advocating on his behalf. He also entertained the delusion that Harrison, if elected to a fifth term, would provide him with a good government job for the work that he had done advocating for him. It is likely that, had he seen a psychiatrist of the time, he would have been diagnosed as a paranoid.

At the end of October another potential obstacle to the fair loomed as threat of an economic recession circulated from London and started to affect American markets. Organizers worried about the cost of the fair as well as concerns that fewer would be able to attend the event due to an impending downturn in the economy, and attendance was a critical measure in terms of the competition with the French exposition. During this period, Burnham was officially appointed as the chief of construction for a fee of $360,000 and he appointed Root the supervising architect, and Olmsted the supervising landscape architect. Still, there was no location.

By the end of 1886, Holmes's pharmacy was doing well. He was also occupied with somewhat of an obsession over Myrta Z. Belknap whom he had met in Minneapolis earlier that year. What attracted him most was a neediness about her that suggested vulnerability. He found the women that had acclimated to urban life to have been hardened wizened in a way that was less attractive to him. He much preferred the women that were new and naïve, not unlike the cities Madams who were known to greet such women at the station. He returned to Minneapolis a few times a month to court her. He violated the rules of courtship brazenly but without shame and so she assumed that perhaps the rules in Chicago were different. He proposed, she accepted, and they married in January of 1887. Two weeks later he filed a motion to prosecute Clara Lovering for divorce with the charge of infidelity. It was later dismissed after he failed to complete the divorce. Myrta moved into the apartment above the pharmacy and was pregnant by spring of 1888.

Myrta began to see a great ambition in the character of her husband, but not in a way that interfered with other qualities. She described him as a man with a gentle heart who loved animals and children. He was also kind in the home and, according to Myrta, never said anything unkind to her or her mother or their daughter. Tension in the marriage did, however, build as Myrta grew increasingly jealous of the single women that insisted on being attended to by her husband in private. He handled her by confining her to the books, and eliminating her from interactions with customers. She wrote her parents of her isolation and they moved to Wilmette, Illinois where she joined them in time to give birth to daughter Lucy. She stayed with her parents and they accepted the increasingly infrequent visits from the doctor but were convinced that his ambition drove him to work long hours in Chicago and were assuaged by the money, gifts and warmth he brought when he did visit.

He bought the lot across the street from the pharmacy in the summer of 1888. He also began to plan the structure that he wanted to construct without the help of an architect. The plans were elaborate and strange. The first floor would be a large storefront where he would employ many women. Apartments were on the second and third floor along with his office on the corner of the second floor. There would be a greased chute from the street leading to his basement where various hidden chambers would be built. Stranger still was his plan for an asbestos lined room adjacent to his office fitted with gas jets. Those jets, as well as others in the house, would be controlled from a panel hidden in his closet.

Soon he had laborers working on the structure. He often insulted the workers on their poor workmanship, refusing to pay them. He fired many, and others quit. This was a calculated plan. It took more time to construct the building, but it kept the cost of the building down while keeping the secrets of the building known to only a handful of people. One bricklayer later said that Holmes propositioned him to drop a stone on another man he claimed to be his brother in law while working on the site. The story cannot be verified, but the author maintains it is consistent with what is known of Holmes.

There were three men that were kept on throughout the construction process and beyond. Charles Chappell started as a laborer but was kept on for other jobs detailed later. He lived near Cook County Hospital and was a machinist by trade. Patrick Quinlan would later move in to the building as its caretaker. Benjamin Pitezel was a carpenter that joined the crew in 1889. Holmes bailed Pitezel out of jail on a charge of forging checks. His role in the Holmes saga would be dramatic. During the construction of the building, Jack the Ripper's reign of terror in London was happening. Holmes read the stories with great interest.

The building was near completion by May of 1890 and Holmes sold the pharmacy and moved in. The store fronts were inviting, one of which was a pharmacy. There was also a restaurant and a barber shop as well as other retail space. The second and third floors held thirty-five, and thirty-six rooms respectively. He also furnished the building with fixtures bought on credit under the same alias used for the deed, H. S. Campbell. One man, C. E. Davis, who was an employee of Holmes described him as very smooth and charismatic, which was a skill that allowed him to continue to avoid creditors. He also claimed that Holmes had the money to pay his debts from the considerable profits from his many, often fraudulent, business endeavors. One woman that did Holmes laundry claimed he offered to give her $6000 to allow him to open a life insurance policy with him as the beneficiary. His explanation to her was that he would profit in the long run from the arrangement. She considered the offer but ultimately declined.

Finally, in November of 1890, the board settled on the Jackson Park location for the fair, with additional exhibits throughout downtown Chicago, Washington Park, and Midway Boulevard. The announcement pleased Holmes greatly for in addition to adding immediate value to his real estate and retail investments, it would bring him in close proximity to plenty of potential victims.

Ironically, despite an over six month delay in reaching a location decision, the board demanded a sketch of plans for the fair within twenty-four hours of making the decision. Burnham and his team, with a reminder to the board that the French designers had at least a year of considering the site before getting to this stage of their plan, produced a rough design that was immediately approved by the board. The main area for the fair was to be about a mile square area near the lake, included hundreds of buildings, a tower of some sort that would rival the Eiffel Tower, and five colossal buildings that together would constitute the Grand Court.

Everyone knew that the project was huge, and the deadline was extremely tight, and in typical Chicago style, everyone felt up to the challenge. However, likely only the top architects really understood the gravity of the variety of serious logistical and environmental challenges that would have to be addressed. For example, rail would need to be constructed throughout the site to transport building materials, police, fire and ambulance services would need to be organized and housed, quarters for the working crews built, and trash and manure removed.

Another issue that soon presented itself concerned the contentious nature of selecting the additional architects needed for the project. Three of the architects chosen by Burnham were from, of all places, New York City: Charles McKim, Richard M. Hunt and George B. Post. The other two included Henry Van Brunt from Kansas City and Robert Peabody from Boston. They were all well-known at the time for being extremely talented architects, but the choice to not include a single other architect from Chicago would draw more criticism than Burnham was prepared for.

On December 15, 1890, Burnham boarded a train for New York to meet with all but Van Brunt who was the only architect that so far had explicitly agreed to his invitation to join the team. Despite his contacts and credibility in New York, Olmsted was not able to join Burnham on the trip due to the work already underway for the landscaping of the grounds. What he did not realize was that these architects from the east had already met in private to discuss their concerns about putting their names on a project that might end up looking like a giant county fair and an embarrassment to the nation.

Hunt, Post, McKim and Peabody met with Burnham over dinner on December 22. All of these men had ties through their formidable formal educations that joined them in a kind of brotherhood, while Burnham was the only man of the group with a mediocre educational background. Burnham was unprepared for the level of skepticism and frank cynicism expressed by the other architects, in particular Hunt. He pressed on and focused on the idea that the fair would shape American ideas about the importance of architecture. He emphasized the resolve of those in Chicago to make the dream a reality despite the hurdles and the fact that they had the capital to make it financially solvent. He was able to break through the initial resistance, and found beneath it a host of questions for which he had no clear answers, and indeed, wanted the help of these talented men to solve. They also expressed concerns that they would be hampered by the huge bureaucracy of the fair, and to this Burnham offered a promise of creative authority.

Burnham left the meeting with only one acceptance, that of Peabody, while the rest agreed to think it over and meet in Chicago on January 10. In the meantime, Root would need to go to New York to participate in the recruitment efforts by making his competence as supervising architect known to them. It would also be critical to cajole Olmsted into being present at the January 10 meeting as his confidence in the project was likely one of the deciding factors for the others. Also, upon returning to Chicago, Burnham found that there was significant hostility over the fact that he had chosen eastern architects, and under pressure to make amends for that he agreed to add five Chicago firms, including Adler & Sullivan. Sullivan still remained somewhat bitter that it was Burnham, and not him, chosen for the chief architect to begin with.

The day that the architects visited the Jackson Park site was windy and cold, increasing the effect of the desolate and dessert like environment of the area. The water was grey, the trees without leaves, and it seemed to be a wasteland. It was a mere twenty-seven and a half months before the congressional act required them to be installing the final exhibits. The architects were gloomy and discouraged. They met with Root back at the Rookery who had enough enthusiasm to perk their spirits some. Root did not attend that night's lavish dinner, intended to demonstrate to the architects from the east that Chicago was perfectly adept at going big. The president of the exposition, Lyman Gage, offered a speech and a toast to bolster the men's confidence in their endeavor. The Chicagoans were roused by the affair, the eastern architects remained gloomy and defeated despite having formally accepted their posts.

Meanwhile, Holmes began modifying his building to make it ready to serve as a hotel for the fair. He also took out a large fire insurance policy. His plan was to burn it down after the fair destroying evidence of his activities as well as generating a hefty profit. He planned to use the same techniques of securing credit in the name of H. S. Campbell, or secured against the Warner Glass Bending Company, and then not paying the creditors. Only if he sensed that creditors would pursue legal or physical action did he pay them, in cash, from his many business ventures. He also swindled Myrta's great-uncle Belknap into financing a home for him and Myrta, then forged his signature on another lien.

Belknap never fully trusted Holmes. After being pressured by both Holmes and Myrta, he relented to a visit to Holmes's property in Englewood, which was at the time only occupied by Holmes and Quinlan. Holmes tried to convince him to visit the roof, but he refused. That night while trying to sleep, he heard someone try to get into his room. He called out and Quinlan answered saying that he wanted to come in, but Belknap refused and the matter was dropped. He soon discovered the forgery as well, but accepted Holmes's graveling that the act was a desperate act forced by his dire economic circumstances.

Holmes also commissioned a device that would act as a cremation chamber for his victims under the guise that it would be a kiln for the Warner Glass Bending Company. Despite having visited the "kiln" in Holmes's basement, an expert furnace builder did not question its purpose despite its odd shape for a glass bending apparatus, and its odd location, in the basement of a structure an entire block in dimension that looked more like a cavern than a glass shaping workshop.

Holmes started visiting Wilmette less often again. He continued to send money so that his wife and daughter were comfortable. He also took out a life insurance policy on his daughter. The drugstore and a mail order drug business were running well, although the young and attractive women that worked at his counter had, recalls on neighbor, a penchant for running off leaving even their belongings behind, understood as typical in the new age of anonymity offered in urban life.

Holmes had a new employee, jewler Icilius "Ned" Conner, who worked the counter at the Sixty-third and Wallace drugstore. He brought with him Julia, his wife, and Pearl, his eight year old daughter. His career and life seemed to be on the brink of a great rise, particularly given the proximity of the establishment to the upcoming World's Columbian Exposition. The family lived in an apartment near Holmes's office on the second floor. Soon Julia's sister Gertrude joined them and was also employed by Holmes. Ned found that in short order, however, the attention that Holmes directed at his wife and sister-in-law captured their attention in a way that made him feel isolated and uncomfortable.

Because of both inadequate police forces, and the sheer volume of missing persons, letters from concerned families on the disappearances of young women, rarely went fully investigated. In addition, there were class dimensions that meant people of lower classes were simply not considered of enough value to invest significant investigative resources in. Unclaimed and unidentified bodies were regularly found. It was simply assumed that the levels of vanished people was a normal part of urban living.

At the final meeting on January 12, before the architects returned home, Burnham told them that they would be a Board of Architects. They chose Hunt as the chairman of the board, and Sullivan as the Secretary. Meanwhile, Root missed the meeting, and was shortly diagnosed with pneumonia. The board continued to meet for the next several days, despite the absence of Burnham who attended to Root, and Hunt, who was bedridden from a severe attack of gout. They made progress refining the plan already offered by Burnham and Root, and decided on some key unifying features of the main architectural plans.

Root passed away on Thursday, January 15, 1891. Burnham was stunned by the loss. When the word got out, the press went wild and speculated that the exposition might be in danger of failing. Burnham considered quitting the fair project, but on the following Monday was back at his desk. Instead, following the announcement of another bank failure, this time in Kansas City, the president of the fair, Lyman Gage, resigned his post so he could focus on the operations of his own bank. The future for the Great Columbian Exhibition looked bleak indeed.

PART II: An Awful Fight, Chicago, 1891-93

The architects met again, along with famous sculpture, Augustus St. Gaudens, on February 24, 1891. They were joined in the afternoon by the Grounds and Buildings Committee, as well as Lyman Gage, who was still serving as president of the exhibition. As the architects unveiled their drawings for the various components of the fair, a sense of overall cohesion of grand vision became apparent. In several places, individual architects realized that elements of their designs might overshadow other buildings and agreed to scale down this feature or that to bring the overall scene into harmony. What became clear to everyone was the sheer ambition of the plans, and the desperately short time left in which to execute them.

The official work on the site commenced on February 11 when immigrant workers began digging a drainage ditch and 500 union workers chased them off the grounds. The crowd of union workers grew to 2,000 men in the coming days. The firm that hired the workers, McArthur Brothers, met with police and union organizers and hammered out a deal that limited work day hours and mandated union wages and preferential hiring. Labor struggles would be an ongoing feature of the fair's construction. There was also a tension between the various administrative bodies, in particular between the Exposition Company made up of private businesses and head by Lyman Gage, and The National Commission which was made up of politicians and led by Director-General George Davis. They argued over control of the details of the project on various levels. Various committees were also established and sometimes had disputes over jurisdictional issues, adding delays.

Compromises for the sake of time were made. One included the use of "staff" which was a composite material used rather than real stone for the building facades and columns. Burnham also hired Charles B. Atwood to replace Root for his designing prowess. Atwood was unreliable due to an opium addiction, but Burnham saw within him a genius. A

Lieutenant Schufeldt was dispatched to the Zanzibar interior to collect a tribe of Pygmies recently discovered there for one of the fair exhibits.

Gertrude suddenly wanted to leave for home, clearly in great distress but unwilling to provide details. She was suddenly nervous around Holmes. She packed her things and left. Customers speculated about a relationship between Holmes and Julia, although Ned denied any signs of it. He was also kept from seeing the full truth by an offer that Holmes made to sell Ned the pharmacy, and Holmes was even gracious enough to handle all of the logistical and legal details. He also offered to buy the whole family life insurance policies and had a friend C. W. Arnold come to consult, but Ned refused the insurance. Holmes did transfer ownership of the pharmacy to Ned, along with all of the debts secured against it and soon creditors were coming after Ned who now owed incredible sums of money. Ned began to suspect Holmes may indeed be having an affair with his wife and tensions between Julia and Ned rose until he left and moved to Gilman, Illinois. He filed for divorce some time later. Pearl and Julia remained with Holmes. However, once Ned was gone, Holmes's interest in Julia and Pearl waned.

Carter Henry Harrison, who had become associated with organized labor, lost the mayoral election in 1891 to a Republican, Hempstead Washburne. Patrick Prendergast, somewhere in the city, was crestfallen that his hero had lost, given hope only by the fact that the loss was by a narrow margin. He committed himself to do even more in the coming years to help Harrison win a fifth term.

Problems at the building site for the fair started to emerge. Testing of the soil showed most of the land was capable of supporting buildings with the floating foundation method that Root had designed. However, the area for the largest building, the Manufactures and Liberal Arts Building would not and the only solution would be to dig supports down to the rock bed, an expensive and time consuming complication. Delays and complications continued to plague Burnham. All of the architectural drawings were late. The final drawings would not be collected until midsummer. Olmsted fell ill and his work slowed. Problems with the rising and falling levels of water created problems for the landscaping team. Still, they used manure from the stockyards to enrich the soil and ordered a gargantuan amount of plants and bulbs from nurseries and expeditions to Lake Calumet.

Sixteen months before dedication day, construction on the first building began. In addition to the buildings of the Grand Court, each state of the nation had its own buildings planned. Two hundred companies combined with several foreign governments also vied for exhibition space on the grounds. Still no idea had been decided on to rival the Eiffel Tower, a critical component of the fair. The *Tribune* hosted a competition for an idea, and several people offered implausible but creative ideas, mostly variations on taller and more spectacular Towers. Burnham thought that another tower could only be imitation, however.

Burnham was ahead of his time in solving several potential problems the fair faced. He insisted on a large police force called the Columbian Guard and appointed Colonel Edmund Rice, an accomplished veteran officer, to be in charge of the outfit. Prevention of crime was as much as part of the focus as catching criminals and arresting them. He also made sure that fire hydrants were plentiful and a fire department which went into operation during the construction phase were on hand to quell any fires. Bacteriology was still in its infancy, however, the Chicago water supply was known to be of poor quality, causing occasional outbreaks of cholera that plagued the city. Fear that a cholera outbreak would taint the reputation of the fair, Burnham had a plant built on the premises to boil and sterilize the water supplying the fairgrounds and made further plans to have spring water pumped in for the fair.

Along with the ongoing political quagmires, labor struggles, and committee interference of all kinds, came the inevitable accidental deaths of builders on the site. In December, four deaths, one by electrocution and the others from head injuries, occurred. Banks continued to fail across the country as well. Despite being drastically behind schedule and amidst all of these forces working against the successful completion of the fair, Burnham kept up with an optimistic public presence.

November of 1891 brought pregnancy for Julia Conner. Holmes agreed to marry her, but only on the condition that she allow him to conduct an abortion given that right now was not a time for children given all of the work that needed doing before the fair. He chose Christmas Eve as the date for the procedure. When that night came, Julia spent time with another family in the building decorating a tree and talking of her upcoming visit with some relatives. Afterwards she joined Holmes in a room where he had a surgical table along with many surgical tools set up, many more than would be required for an abortion. He then put her to sleep with chloroform, following with more until she was dead. He then went to Pearl's room, and did the same.

The family with the tree expected to see Pearl and Julia the next morning, but they never arrived. When they enquired with Holmes he stated that she had left for her trip early. They and other tenants thought it odd. Meanwhile, Holmes summoned Charles Chappell, an associate who had practice with "articulating" which meant stripping the muscle from bone and then assembling the skeleton for use in medical offices and classrooms. This desire for specimens was outpacing demand, and grave robbing became one method of securing bodies that doctors had learned to turn a blind eye to as a means to procure the needed specimens. Bodies were always in demand for dissection, experimentation, and eventually articulation. Chappell arrived to find a body with the skin stripped off the flesh. Holmes told him that he had completed his experiments and offered Chappell $36 to articulate the skeleton and he agreed. The body was shipped to his home in a trunk by an express shipping company. When the skeleton was complete, Holmes sold it to Hahneman Medical Collage and pocketed a tidy profit. In January of 1892, Holmes moved the Doyle family into Julia's old room, with her belongings untouched. He told them that she left on family emergency and would not be returning, later refining the story to suggest the Iowa destination was a ruse to throw off her husband who pursued custody of their daughter.

By 1892 the treasury for the coffers of the Exposition Company were diminishing rapidly. A plan for asking the national congress for an appropriation was underway, but in the meantime cost cuts must be made. Labor was the easiest to cut and Burnham was forceful with the leaders of the various crews to fire the most expensive men, and those that showed any signs of slacking on the job. Previously known for fair work practices, Burnham recognized that there was now no choice.

Still no design for a centerpiece to rival the Eiffel Tower emerged. There was a group of fair engineers that met each Saturday called the Saturday Club. One weekend Burnham joined them and gave a speech admonishing American engineers for failing to rise fully to the challenge of the fair and produce a marvel worthy of showcasing American engineering. One engineer at the talk was convinced that Burnham was right, and an idea came to him that he thought sure was grand enough to put Eiffel to shame.

Tension between Burnham and Director-General Davis mounted. The commission continued to sprout new departments and committees, taking control over things that Burnham felt squarely fell under his jurisdiction. To add insult to injury, Davis claimed that should federal monies come through, they should be controlled by the commission. A particular battle ground was control over the exhibits. When the congressional money did come, it also triggered an oversight investigation of expenditures, culminating in an altercation between the two men in front of a congressional subcommittee meeting concerning the total cost of the fair.

Sol Bloom, a young accomplished man with a background in theater operations, was hired to manage that Midway section of the fair. This area would be devoted to "alien" and "primitive" cultures. His goal, in opposition to Professor Putnam, an ethnologist originally in charge of the area, was to make the site a source of entertainment speckled with shock. He had a knack for advertisement and promotion, and soon other organizers from the fair sought his help.

Holmes, meanwhile, sent his associate Pitezel to a facility in Dwight, Illinois that specialized in the Keeley cure for alcoholism, and paid for the treatments which included daily injections of a mysterious and highly guarded concoction. Of course his motives also included getting as much information on the Keeley cure as possible so that he could imitate the cure and sell it. While at the facility, Pitezel met a woman named Emeline Cigrand that worked there. Upon hearing of this woman and her great beauty from Pitezel, Holmes offered her twice the salary to come work for him, which she accepted. He immediately began courting her. They took many bicycle rides, as was the fashion of the day, including many to the site of the fair under construction. He told her he was the son of an English Lord, but that it was a closely guarded secret. He proposed to her and she accepted enthusiastically.

October 21, 1892 was the planned day for the dedication ceremony for the World's Fair, and yet by spring the grounds seemed impossibly far from construction goals. Olmsted in particular found the delays frustrating since landscaping around the buildings could not be completed until they were finished. Olmsted also had to rebuff repeated attacks from a variety of parties who wanted to build on the Wooded Island that he insisted must be free of manmade structures. He finally relented to the Japanese contingent who wanted to build beautiful temples in harmony with the natural surroundings and to leave the buildings behind after the fair. In addition, his health steadily declined. He put his young colleague Codman in charge of the grounds while he planned to take rest in Europe. Meanwhile, Bloom received word that his Algerian tribe had left France for America a year ahead of schedule. A windstorm that spring destroyed some of the structures that were under construction, adding further delays.

The water purification system installed by Burnham would not meet the demands of so many people once the fair was underway. In addition, a storm caused the reverse of the Chicago River which threatened the safety of the water supply. Burnham needed to finish his plan of piping water in from the Waukesha spring. He had a contract with Hygeia Mineral Springs Company, but progress seemed to have slowed to a near halt with a fast approaching deadline. The president of the company, J. E. McElroy, had encountered trouble with the locals concerned that his pipeline would mar their geography. He decided to dig the pipe in the middle of the night and had a train take a crew and materials for the dig the evening of May 7, 1892. However, when the train arrived at the station with the men and materials for the dig, a small armed militia and a growing crowd of townspeople turned them back after a short standoff. Fortunately for Burnham, McElroy was able to secure rights from a town just south of Waukesha, still in the same county, and the pipeline proceeded.

A break in the political quagmire came in August when the company and the commission appointed Burnham as director of works, giving him final control over everything, which would significantly streamline the remaining construction. Meanwhile, the young engineer from Pittsburg that was impressed by Burham's speech at the Saturday Club worked out the formal specifications for the contraption that would rival Eiffel, and Burnham along with the Ways and Means Committee approved the plan. The committee revoked approval the next day. A few months later, backed by investors prepared to pay for his project, the engineer once again approached the board and was finally approved. The engineer from Pittsburgh, George Washington Gale Ferris, commissioned Luther V. Rice to be the supervising engineer in Chicago for the construction of his 250 foot vertical, revolving wheel.

Olmsted returned to a changed landscape in September and the final rush to install temporary landscaping to suffice for the dedication ceremony began. The giant 32 acre building, the Manufactures and Liberal Arts Building, housed 140,000 people for the dedication ceremony. Many would not actually hear the proceedings because of the immensity of the space, and a lack of microphone technology. The press was overall kind and celebratory of the affair. Work then continued on the fairgrounds in anticipation of opening day.

In another part of the city, Patrick Prendergast filled out a postcard addressed to Alfred S. Trude, a prominent Chicago attorney. On it he offered condolences concerning a recent accident the lawyer was in, along with some other tangential prose concerning how the final arbitrator of the law is Jesus Christ, and his opinions on the most important commandments of God. He left no room to sign the card.

Over the months Mrs. Lawrence, a tenant in the Holmes building, and Emeline became close confidants. A few weeks before Christmas, Mrs. Lawrence was surprised to find out that Emeline was planning a trip to see family, and may not be coming back. It seemed that her feelings had been changing for Holmes, perhaps in retrospect as she learned more of his true nature. In any event, shortly thereafter she disappeared without even saying goodbye to the Lawrence's which struck them as odd and disconcerting. When they asked Holmes about it, he responded that she had eloped with a man and that he was the only person that new of their secret. A few days later, unsatisfied, she asked again and he produced a wedding announcement, one that was also similarly mailed to some family and friends. Mrs. Lawrence was still unsatisfied and later recalled strange behavior following her disappearance that included Holmes locked in his office for the better part of the day with only Quinlan being allowed in, followed by an express carriage that came to take away a trunk so heavy it took two additional male tenants to lift. She felt sure that he had killed her, although she did not contact police, nor did she and her husband move.

When Emeline's trunk of personal affects arrived at the train station in her parent's hometown, they did not know what to make of it. Her correspondence, a few times a week since she had left home, immediately dropped to nothing after the marriage announcement. They speculated that perhaps she had died and that her new husband lacked information on how to contact them. It turns out that Phelps, the name given on the wedding announcement, was the alias used by Pitezel at Dwight where he met Emeline. Once again, Holmes contracted Chappell to articulate the bones and Holmes sold them, this time to LaSalle Medical College. Three years later police would discover a footprint etched into the door of the soundproof room in Holmes's office, probably etched by acid that was thrown on the floor to accelerate depleting the oxygen in the room while Emeline struggled to live and escape her fate.

The winter that started 1893 was bitter cold. The grounds were far behind and Opening Day was a meager four months away. Ferris had to use dynamite to crack the frozen crust of ground for construction of his wonder. Problems continued in terms of dealing with the quicksand layers and pouring concrete in twenty degrees below zero temperatures. Because of his considerable contacts in the steel trade, given that his company focused on steel-inspection services, he was able to procure the necessary raw materials for the structure. He also had the pull to have each piece inspected right on the line, which was a critical advantage for the 100,000 component steel monstrosity. The weight of the axel alone, which was made in a single cast at Bethlehem Steel, was 142,031 pounds, the heaviest object ever raised, and would need to be lifted to the top of eight 140 foot towers.

Codman, admitted to the hospital for acute appendicitis, died. Olmsted, plagued by his own health issues, had no choice but to completely take over the landscaping operations of the fair to have it prepared for opening day. By February 17, Olmsted was placed on confinement in his hotel under doctor's orders. The landscaping supervision went to Rudolf Ulrich, Olmsted's superintendent, but the relationship was one of distrust, mainly because of Ulrich's pension for getting lost in details and losing sight of the larger picture.

Two months from Opening Day a snow storm laid so much snow that the roof of the Manufacturers and Liberal Arts Building collapsed.

By the early months of 1893, Holmes was doing well. He had several successful business operations. In addition to his thriving retail and rental businesses he had added partial stake in a company that made machines which could copy documents, and the Silver Ash Institute, an alcohol treatment business. He had two homes, one where wife Myrta and daughter Lucy lived, and the other on Honoré Street. And, the fair would soon come bringing a boom of customers and temporary tenants. He did not expect he would be staying long in Chicago after the fair, however. Mrs. Lawrence was persistent with her questions, and the creditors were becoming more aggressive. Parents of the Conner Cigrand women had hired private detectives to follow up on their vanished daughters. For now, Holmes felt confident that he was not a suspect and handled the detective's questions with ease.

In March he was joined by Minnie R. Williams, a young heiress he met in Boston years earlier and she was a perfect match for his taste in women which included a sense of isolation and need. He had met and courted her in Boston under the alias Harry Gordon. She loved him. What he loved was her intense expressions of need before he would leave to return to Chicago. However, it eventually became tiring for him and so he stopped correspondence. She returned to her life and finished school but was drawn to Chicago both for her love of Harry, and the exciting allure of the World's Fair. When she arrived, she contacted him and he immediately came and showered her with affection and invited her to come work for him under the stipulation that she understood that H. H. Holmes was his business alias and how he was known in Chicago.

She moved in to one of the apartments in his building after a short stay in a nearby boarding house. He proposed, and she accepted, writing of the news eagerly to her sister, Anna. Before they were to be married, he convinced her to transfer the considerable Texas estate that she had inherited to a man named Alexander Bond (one of his aliases) and then in turn to Benton T. Lyman (an alias for Pitezel). The marriage was a simple affair, insisted on by Holmes, and in fact, was never registered legally.

At the fairgrounds, exhibits began arriving spring of 1893. Despite an economic downturn that was affecting the country, the local economy was solid, in large part due to the activity of the fair. The steel for the Ferris Wheel came on five trains, each with thirty cars. Great military machines arrived for display including a replica of the British warship *Victoria*, and a 250,000 pound German artillery gun. Buffalo Bill and his troupe for the Wild West show, including nearly 100 American Indians and former Calvary soldiers who set up camp adjacent to the fair since they had been denied formal inclusion into the fair itself. Sphinxes and Mummies arrived along with exotic animals such as ostriches, monkeys and camels. People from far off and exotic places also arrived including supposed cannibals from Dahomey, and people from Cairo, Lapland and Syria, all coming to inhabit special exhibits displaying their cultures and customs. The Pygmies, incidentally, did not arrive. Unfortunately Lieutenant Schufeldt died, for reasons unknown. Bloom, who had opened his exhibit the previous August, had found many opportunities to make money at other venues with his Algerian belly dancing troupe.

Critics across the nation offered advice in newspaper columns. Blue-bloods from New York lifted their noses high in the air and pontificated on the lack of French chefs at the affair, and the proper way to frappe wine, triggering the working class insecurities of Chicagoans and striking at the core of the rivalry between the cities. Chicago papers responded with parodies mocking the snobbery. In truth, however, Burnham's own aesthetic was guided by his own experiences in running in circles where he was nearly the only man without a high pedigree of an Ivy League education, so it would be unfair to say that the higher class expectations did not drive the overall sensibilities of the fair.

Of graver concern, however, was the state of the cleanliness of the city. A New York journalist by the name of Jacob Riis, committed to speaking for the squalid living conditions of the poor in America, came to Chicago and after a tour gave a talk at the Hull House. He reported that the streets of Chicago were far worse than any in New York and that fixing such a disgrace ought to be a priority. Chicago had already been working on this issue but to mixed degrees of success. Organized crime from madam's to gangsters was also a concern for the city. The author notes that Carter Henry Harrison, in his four mayoral terms, had helped such business ventures get established. Since his loss in the last election he had purchased the *Chicago Times* and had rallied enough support to be the "Fair Mayor." While certainly very popular with working men, Harrison was a symbol of a Chicago that people like Burnham wanted to fade away. The white buildings of the fair itself, the White City, symbolized a future for the town where vice driven business would be driven further underground in favor of legitimate leadership. Still, Harrison was gaining ground in advance of the upcoming election.

Prendergast believed this new gain in momentum was due in no small part to his own work in soliciting for his hero in his postcard campaign. He also became more invested in the idea that Harrison was surely in his debt, and that upon his reelection, Harrison would repay his gratitude with a handsome job opportunity. He thought an appointed position as corporation counsel would be a good fit for his talents, finally raising him out of the dirty streets of Chicago and liberating him for a life where the newsboys that worked for him failed to see and appreciate his genius for business. His cards were sent to men of high classes but used a familiarity of tone that made his cards stand out as troubling amidst the piles of mail that such men received. In April 1893, Harrison won the mayoral election. Prendergast failed to register on Harrison's to-do list.

When Minnie told her sister Anna about the transfer of ownership of her inherited land, Holmes suspected that Anna was growing distrustful of his motives. He had Minnie invite her for a visit for an all-expense paid trip to the World's Fair. Anna accepted and Minnie was ecstatic.

By April of 1893, preparations for the fair had reached a feverish pitch. The worker death toll, however, had risen to seven for 1893 alone. A last minute labor strike slowed progress some, but the weather was gorgeous which shored up Burnham's resolve and confidence. The grand buildings were all but finished, and the effect was spectacular. The 111 foot tall "Statue of the Republic" was complete and in place. The roof on the Manufactures and Arts Building was repaired and the space within was grand indeed. Independent labor had been sufficient to minimize the effects of the union strike. The exotic birds that Olmsted ordered were installed and seemed to be doing well. Buffalo Bill opened his show, on 15 acres adjacent to the fairgrounds, on April 3 to sold-out crowds of 18,000.

It did become apparent to Burnham that, after labor became more organized and threatened a wider strike, he would have to negotiate with union leaders. He did and the agreement that was put in place established a minimum wage, daily hour limits, and time and a half for overtime and holidays. The agreement struck would later be used as a template for future labor disputes and it bolstered the general support for the power of unions to improve working conditions for working men.

On April 18 a rain began to fall. At first there was no worry as the grounds, particularly all the newly planted flowers, shrubs and other greenery could use it. However, the rain continued and by nightfall it was pouring in great torrents. Leaks formed in the roof of the giant Manufactures and Liberal Arts Building and dumped water on the exhibits within. Over the next few days the rain continued, shorting circuits, making a muddy mess of campsites and exterior villages, and finding its way through the roof of the Women's Building as well. Little dips in the roads became large puddles, worsened by the wheels of carriages. Despite poor health, Olmsted worked tirelessly to oversee the work of the landscaping.

The deadline fast approached. Even a few days before the opening ceremony, much remained to be done. The president of the United States, Grover Cleveland, would soon lead a parade procession to the grounds. Hundreds of important dignitaries, cabinet officials, leaders of industry and celebrities the world over were checking into the finest hotels and readying for the ceremony. Meanwhile, British reporter F. Herbert Stead made a trip in the pouring rain to the fairgrounds on the eve of the opening ceremony and found a disheartening scene of incompleteness, with materials and trash from workers still strewn about the grounds littered with muddy puddles.

PART III: IN THE WHITE CITY, MAY-OCTOBER 1893

On May 1, 1893, a carriage procession with President Cleveland, royalty, dignitaries and statesmen, with Mayor Harrison in the last car led 200,000 people on foot, horseback and streetcars into the park for the opening ceremony. The Columbian Guard, in full dress uniforms, marched 1,500 strong. The sun peaked out just as the procession arrived at the grounds to an ecstatic cheer of the crowd. The path of the procession went along the Midway Plaisance and beside the Ferris Wheel, still incomplete. The multicultural exhibits along the Midway all made their own special nod to the President as his carriage passed, including the roar of trained lions in the zoo.

Most importantly, the scene of dishevelment witnessed by Stead just the night before had been tidied quite efficiently by the 10,000 workers that worked through the night in the rain. Although still not complete, the landscaping passed muster despite the fact that some areas were underwater from the torrential and unrelenting rains. The President took his seat on the stage at 11:00 a.m. The ceremony was kept short, due likely to the criticism that the longer dedication ceremony had drawn. A few songs followed by a speech from Director-General Davis preceded the President's address. President Cleveland's invocation was short and at the end he turned a key and a simultaneous flutter of activity followed. Engines across the park suddenly came to life creating a hum that was palpable. Fountains shooting water hundreds of feet into the air came to life, the canvas dropped from the great golden statue nicknamed "Big Mary," huge flags unfurled in every direction, and the *Michigan* fired its guns. Somewhere in the crowd, the famous feminist philanthropist Jane Addams felt for her purse only to realize it was stolen. The World's Columbian Exposition had officially begun.

Despite the remaining work of finishing the landscaping and the Ferris Wheel, congratulations on the success of the fair to meet the expectations of the nation poured in, much to Burnham's relief. The numbers of attendees on opening day are a matter of some contention, but range between 250,000 to 620,000, and suggested that the World's Fair would be the most attended entertainment venue in history. The next day, however, only 10,000 attended, which indicated the fair would be a huge failure. On May 3, a Wall Street panic overshadowed the fair, followed by a series of financial failures in the following weeks across the nation that stifled travel dramatically. Burnham set about finishing the fairgrounds and placed Frank Millet in charge of promoting the park to lure attendees. The efforts had minimal effect, and the economy continued to decline.

Meanwhile, Holmes had named his establishment at Sixty-third and Wallace "The World's Fair Hotel." The volume of guests was not what he and others had hoped for, but their proximity near Jackson Park did lure customers. Holmes politely told male customers that he lacked vacancies to save his rooms for young women unused to the ways of urban life. Minnie grew increasingly jealous and clingy so Homes put a deposit on a lavish apartment far enough away to keep her at bay on the pretense that since they were now married they needed a nicer place to live. The elegance of the flat pleased Millie and the couple moved in, although Holmes himself stayed largely at his hotel, managing affairs. The women at the hotel appreciated his kindness and attention, and the fact that the whole place smelled vaguely of a doctor's office due to the ever present chemical smells seemed consistent with the fact that a pharmacy was downstairs. He was perceived as a forgiving and gentle man who did not make a fuss when some women checked out suddenly without paying their bill.

Prendergast wrote a card to a W. F. Cooling informing him that upon his appointment to corporation counsel he would select Cooling as his assistant.

There was a deep contrast provided by the White City of the fairgrounds and the Black City of Chicago. Many came to see the White City as the future of urban life. Technological innovations displayed at the fair were marvels of invention yet unfamiliar to the attendees. A live concert in New York was transmitted by telephone. The Kinetoscope invented by Edison showed moving pictures. Tesla did spectacular displays of electricity. Electric appliances of all kinds, novel foods produced using mass production techniques, and the prevalence of electric lighting all raised awe among spectators.

Weather improved and remained good throughout the summer, and the grounds in general improved. The Court of Honor which showcased the great buildings designed by the architectural team was a site of particular magnificence for many visitors. The decision to keep the cornices at the same height proved to unite the buildings into a spectacle of wonder. The white paint further joined them into a harmony. The light at different times of day had a particularly dramatic effect as the color of the buildings shifted in unison with the rising and setting sun. At night the electric lights that filled each building and lined each walkway were dazzling. Even the building exteriors and the fountains were lighted to maximum artistic effect and the results astounded visitors. Reports began to make it to the corners of the nation that visitors in general were not prepared for the wonders they witnessed at the fair and that no words or images could adequately capture the experience of the event. Despite economic concerns, attendance began to rise.

Meanwhile, a waitress in Holmes's restaurant vanished. Followed by a stenographer, then a woman that may have worked for Holmes or may have simply been a tenant, followed by a male physician that rented an office in the building. Holmes answered questions from family and friends of the vanished with a helpful tone. The police, very busy with keeping crime down around the fair and the streets of Chicago, did not get involved. Holmes, distanced himself somewhat from the actual act of killing. Sometimes allowing the gas jets installed in the rooms do the work for him, other times creeping into the room of a sleeping woman and using a rag doused with chloroform. His interest was more in the complete possession of their corpses and it is there that he spent more time with his victims. After he was finished, only a new "acquisition" would sate him.

At 6:00 p.m. on June 9, the Ferris Wheel, standing at 264 feet at its topmost arc, rotated for the first time, although the seats had not yet been installed. The test was successful. The wheel did a full rotation in 20 minutes to a growing crowd of awed onlookers. The following days the 936,000 extra pounds of weight of the cars would be loaded onto the wheel.

Minnie's sister Anna, whom she called "Nannie," arrived in mid-June of 1893. Her suspicions that he may be up to no good faded when she saw that he obviously loved her sister a great deal. They took a tour of the city, followed by a tour of the Union Stock Yards that included a close up view of the killing floor. Then they visited the fair. The author uses this as an opportunity to showcase more of the fair's wonders. In the Manufactures and Liberal Arts Building the largest electric chandeliers ever made hung from the 236 foot ceilings and glowed with 828,000 candlepower. Within the great hall were thousands of exhibits, many of them displays of foreign and domestic goods. It took two weeks of daily visits to get an adequate coverage of the fair for visitors lucky enough to have enough time. They saw the phonograph and the first electric chair. They spent an entire day on the Midway with its exotic and eclectic mix of people and cultural artifacts from around the world. Delighted, Anna accepted Holmes invitation to stay for the summer.

The Ferris Wheel had six cars hung by June 11 and it was ready for its first passenger ride. Among the first were Ferris's assistant in Chicago, Gronau and Ferris's wife. Ferris himself was on urgent unrelated business in New York. Other passengers rushed the deck and eagerly filled the cars with a hundred or more at a time. The wheel was in operation until dark and the following day more cars were hung and the Columbian Guard was called in to keep the clambering crowds at bay. Meanwhile, Olmsted was traveling the country and enquiring about the fair among the many people he encountered. Three main stories predominated. Firstly, among those that had visited the fair, the sentiment was that fair was much more than what the papers had led them to expect. Secondly, much to Olmsted's delight, the grounds themselves were a major part of the experience of the fair's splendor. Thirdly, somewhat more troubling, was the sense that although many people planned to go, they sensed the Fair was yet incomplete and planned to travel to it later so they could have the complete experience.

A small fire broke out on June 17 in the Cold Storage Building that manufactured ice for the fair. Upon inspection after the fact the Fire Marshal realized that a thimble shaped structure at the top of the main furnace tower designed to protect the wood from the heat of the furnace was inexplicably not installed. Insurers as a result cancelled their policies. Burnham was not notified.

On June 21 the Ferris Wheel was officially ready to host passengers and a small ceremony, including a speech by its creator, commemorated the achievement. Mayor Harrison also joined the company into the first car after the ceremony. People were awestruck by the light appearance of the structure. The thin rods seemed fully incapable of supporting the massive weight of the wheel. Concerns were raised among many of the attendees about how the structure would fare in strong winds, a concern that would be tested in a few short weeks.

The end of June showed at last a rising tide of visitors to the fair. Crime was surprisingly low with an average of 16 arrests per day for largely petty theft, pickpocketing and disorderly conduct. The fair's hospital functioned well and oversaw treatments for a typical amount of injuries and afflictions. The overall effect of the fair was one of great pride among Chicagoans. Many citizens of the city shared a pride in the exposition, even when they themselves had nothing to do with its design or construction. It seemed to put an end to the claims from the east that Chicago would always be a second class city associated with organized crime and slaughterhouses. The fair also protected Chicago from the worst of the economic effects of the continuing collapse of American banking.

A grand fireworks display, planned by Frank Millet, was scheduled for the 4th of July. The fireworks did not disappoint.

They were fired from boats, the shoreline and even a manned balloon craft. The crowds roared in waves of delight. Holmes with his Minnie and her sister, attended the event. That night he told the women that he would send them on a trip to Milwaukee, followed by Maine and New York. The women wrote letters home that very night telling family of their plans. The next morning Holmes had Minnie prepare the flat for the next tenant while he took Anna to see his World's Fair Hotel.

Once at the hotel he showed Anna the premises, ending in his office. He sat at his desk and asked her to retrieve some papers from the adjacent room, and she happily complied. He locked the door behind her. She must have thought it was an accident and that he would return because the panic he was waiting for did not set in right away. However, as she ran out of oxygen, he listened carefully to the sounds of her last desperate attempts to live by listening close to the gas pipe. After she went silent, he filled the chamber with gas to be sure that she was dead. He then went to the apartment on Wrightwood and gathered Minnie, telling her that Anna would meet them at the building. A few days later he canceled the lease for the apartment on Wrightwood. He also ordered a special delivery man to pick up a long coffin sized box to drop off at the Depot, and a large trunk to be delivered to Charles Chappell.

On July 9 the balloon operator, noticing a sudden drop in barometric pressure on his instruments, cancelled his remaining flights and noticed the Ferris Wheel operators did not take such precautions. A storm built very rapidly with a small funnel cloud that followed the shoreline towards the fair. Glass shattered in several buildings, including some falling from the roof of the Agriculture building. A section of the roof of the Machinery Building ripped free of its frame. The Ferris Wheel was full of passengers and continued to turn. The hot air balloon ripped free of its tethers and the people on the wheel watched in terror as the wind ripped it to shreds. The Ferris Wheel did survive the storms and rattled passengers disembarked without injury.

The next day, however, the Cold Storage Building again caught fire. This time, however, the fire was not as easily contained, and while several firemen were on the tower working to extinguish the main fire, a hidden fire created by interior chambers burst into explosive flame killing twelve firemen and three of the workers while those on the Ferris Wheel watched on. A crowd also gathered on the lawn outside the building. There was an inquest into the causes of the fire, and on July 18 the jury charged Burnham and the Fire Marshall, as well as two Hercules officers, with criminal negligence. The charges were then sent to a grand jury for review. Burnham maintained that he was never notified of the missing thimble, and that his only responsibility for the building included the final approval of the design, which was clearly not followed during the actual construction. The author does not include details on the eventual resolution of the trial.

Meanwhile, directors of the exposition gave in to pressure from the banks concerned that the fair make profits and created a Retrenchment Committee designed to cut costs in an effort to make sure the fair was profitable. Burnham, released on bond the next day, was convinced that such measures would be the death nail of the fair.

Holmes was soon courting again and brought Georgiana Yoke to the fair. She was from Franklin, Indiana and was-twenty three. Holmes told her stories about owning land in Europe, and that his only living family, an uncle, recently died leaving him land in Texas. He proposed to her at the fair, and she agreed. He convinced her that he would need to use his uncle's name for the marriage, Henry Mansfield Howard, saying that it was a condition of his uncle's will that he change his name thusly.

It was a matter of pride among Chicago businessmen that the fair turn a profit. The Retrenchment Committee reported in late July after some initial investigation that significant cost cuts needed to be put in place immediately. But the committee had over played its hand with too harsh of criticism, and a demand for too much power at a time when the fair was by all other accounts, an astounding success. The members of the board threatened to resign if the committee was further empowered, and when denied the power to act with force, the members of the committee itself resigned. Organizers still knew that attendance would have to increase dramatically for the fair to be financially solvent, however. Early on in the planning, the railroads steadfastly refused to lower fares, but now the directors of the fair tried again. The press too jumped on the band wagon of critiquing the railroads for interfering with the support of such a national pride for the sake of greed. The author does not suggest whether or not a fare decrease ever actually occurred. In addition, Frank Millet continued to invent new attractions such as boating and swimming races between the peoples of the Midway, and a grand ball that included them as central to the festivities. Attendance began to rise.

More banks failed and the ranks among the unemployed grew, and were involved in minor skirmishes with police. Organized labor leaders such as Samuel Gompers articulated more radical sermons on the relations between capital and workers and the business elite were getting nervous.

In the first week of October, Prendergast, disappointed that official news of his appointment had yet to be announced, decided to go visit his future office and introduce himself to the outgoing corporation counsel. He did not leave the meeting very satisfied with the tone of introduction.

October 9 was called Chicago Day at the fair, and people attended in record numbers. In part the attendance was boosted by a declaration by Mayor Harrison for businesses to suspend operations for the day so that Chicagoans could attend the event. The record daily attendance of 397,000 set by the World Fair in Paris, was shattered by noon, and yet people were still arriving. The fireworks planned that night exceeded everyone's wildest expectations. When the tickets were finally counted well after midnight, the attendance that day was 751,026. The next day the trustees of the Exposition Company paid their debt to bankers in full with a $1.5 million check made out to the Illinois Trust and Savings Company. The fair was now officially a profitable venture.

At this point the author turns to the winding down of the fair, and the return to normal life of many of the people that have thus far been included in his narrative. Many expressed some sadness that the fair, slated to be torn down after it closed at the end of October, was destined to be such a temporary thing. Olmsted moved on to his many other projects, including the Biltmore, but knew that his career was winding down. Sullivan and Adler continued their partnerships, but to less success than they had expected. In addition, Sullivan fired one of the youngest members of the team, a Mr. Frank Lloyd Wright, for moonlighting. When work ended on the fair, the ten thousand workers involved in its construction and maintenance joined the growing unemployment lines of the growing recession. The streets of the Black City would, by winter, be more full of despair and violence than ever.

Holmes was ready to leave the city as well given that creditors and family members' pursuits now seemed more relentless than ever. He set a fire to the top floor of his building and filed an insurance claim for H. S. Campbell. The insurance inspector suspected but could not prove arson, but advised the company to pay only to Campbell in person. Under the increased scrutiny of now obliquely accusatory investigators hired by the families of Minnie, Anna, the Cigrands and the Smythes as well as other parents, he would never claim the money. In addition, the insurance investigation made clear the breadth of the credit fraud and the creditors joined forces by hiring a single attorney to represent their combined interests. George B, Chamberlin who would later take credit for being the first to see Holmes as a criminal.

That fall, Chamberlin called Holmes to a meeting where, to his surprise, they were joined by a police officer and as many as two dozen creditors that claimed to have been defrauded. To Chamberlin's amazement, Holmes was able to weave a tale with such sincerity and heartfelt grief of being ruined by the panic of 1893, many of the creditors immediately softened and prepared to negotiate a settlement. Chamberlin asked Holmes to leave the room while he tried to talk sense into his clients. Meanwhile, one of the attorneys left the room to get a drink of water, tipped Holmes off to the fact that the group had again shifted towards arrest, and Holmes was able to flee the scene. Very soon after he left for the property in Texas determined to sell off some of the land, and duplicate his mansion in this new territory. He brought Pitezel with him, although he secured a life insurance policy in his name for $10,000 before leaving Chicago. He also traveled with his new fiancée, Geogianna Yoke.

Closing day fast approached and the organizers of the fair had expectations that it may even surpass Chicago Day in total attendance. Millet planned day long celebrations of many varieties including fireworks, music, speeches and a full size reenactment of the Columbus landing on replica ships that Spain constructed for the fair. However, for Mayor Harrison, the big day would be American Cities Day in which 5,000 mayors from across the country would descend on the fair. He announced that morning of his engagement to Annie Howard. In the afternoon he took to the stage and addressed the mayors, expounding on the virtues of the fair and the great city of Chicago.

At 2:00 p.m. that after noon, Prendergast purchased a revolver. He then tried to see Governor John P. Altgeld, but was denied entry as the building official sensed something seriously wrong with the man. At 7:30 p.m. he knocked on the door of the Harrison mansion asking to see the Mayor. The mayor prided himself on being available to the public and so such random occurrences were not completely unheard of. He was told by the parlor maid to return in half an hour after supper. At exactly 8:00 p.m. he again rang the doorbell and this time was invited to wait in the parlor while the maid fetched the mayor. Within moments, and with no record of the conversation between the men, Prendergast shot the mayor who soon died from the wound. Prendergast then exchanged fire with the mayor's coachman who was not shot, then went on foot to the nearby police station and turned himself in. When asked why he shot the mayor, Prendergast cited that the mayor had not kept his word concerning his appointment to corporation counsel.

The planners cancelled all closing festivities and instead held a memorial service on the fairgrounds. Afterwards the guns of the *Michigan* signaled with a twenty-one gun salute and the flags on the fairgrounds were lowered simultaneously marking the end of the World's Fair.

The fair sat empty that winter, and it became a home for the many homeless whose ranks soared. Fires took some of the buildings, and the statue of Big Mary was chipped and vandalized. Striking continued and more violence erupted in clashes with police. Federal troops moved into Chicago, led in a strange twist of fate, by the former grand marshal of the fair, General Nelson Miles, who would now fight against the same workers that built the fair. In July of 1894, seven of the great buildings were set fire by arsonists, including the

Manufacturers and Arts Building. Another thing became clear after the fair, the numbers of people that vanished during the event was astounding.

PART IV: CRUELTY REVEALED, 1895

In June of 1895, H. H. Holmes resided in the Moyamensing Prison in Philadelphia for insurance fraud. Pinkerton National Detective Agency was hired by Fidelity Mutual Life Association to investigate the increasing amount of evidence suggesting Holmes had faked the death of a policyholder, Benjamin Pitezel. The investigation thus far suggested that after leaving Chicago, Holmes and his accomplice Pitezel had traveled to Fort Worth, St. Louis, and finally Philadelphia, with several frauds en route. The agency then tracked him to Burlington, Vermont and on to Boston and where he was arrested and confessed to the fraud. He was then extradited to Philadelphia where he was now awaiting trial. Since the arrest, it was becoming evident that Holmes had killed Pitezel. Detective Frank Geyer was an experienced Philadelphia detective put on the case, specifically to try to find three of Pitezel's children who remained missing.

Geyer met with Holmes but the interview revealed to him more about Holmes penchant for flamboyant lies, smooth tones, and faked sentimentality wielded to throw the listener off his track. Holmes's story was that he had left a body that would pass for Ben Pitezel in a home and set fire to his upper body with an accelerant so as to obscure the identity of the body. He then helped the coroner identify the body, going so far as to indicate and remove a wart on the neck that he claimed was an identifying feature. Carrie, Pitezel's wife, was too ill to help with the identification and the coroner wanted another family member present. Holmes fetched Alice, the fifteen year old daughter of the man. After the benefit was paid, Holmes convinced Carrie to allow him to take Alice and two of the other children to see their father whom she believed was hiding out. Nellie at age eleven and Howard at age eight, joined Holmes and Alice for the trip. During the trip the girls wrote letters home and when he was arrested, the letters were found among Holmes's possessions, never having been mailed. Holmes later told Carrie that Minnie Williams was caring for the children in London, but authorities there had not located them.

From the children's letters, Geyer was able to surmise that Cincinnati was the first stop on their journey so that is where he started. He visited with the police superintendent to alert him to his search and he received some support from Detective John Schnooks. They visited all of the hotels near the train station until they came to the Atlantic House. There he found in the ledger an entry dated the day that Holmes left St. Louis with the three children. The name of the visitor was Alex E. Cook, which Geyer recognized as an alias that Holmes had used before, and Cook was traveling with three children. He also knew from the letters that despite the fact that Cook was registered for one night at this hotel, they stayed in the city for two nights. They continued their search and found another A. E. Cook entry, again with three children, at the Bristol hotel. The clerk recognized the photographs.

Another lead came from the fact that the Pinkertons had discovered that Holmes often rented homes when he traveled, and so the team pursued that lead to the J. C. Thomas realty agency. It turns out that Holmes left a memorable impression on people because he was often remembered by those that encountered him. He had rented a house the day they arrived in Cincinnati, but only for two days. They interviewed the neighbor who shared something strange. She saw a large stove, she thought far too big for a house, was delivered, but then the next day Holmes cam to tell her that he would not be staying and she could have the stove.

Satisfied that he had all the information he would get out of Cincinnati, Detective Geyer went next to Indianapolis. There he was assigned another temporary partner, Detective David Richards. He immediately recognized a location from one of the letters and the detectives set off for The Hotel English. Three children by the name of Canning were listed in the registry, and Canning was Carrie Pitezel's maiden name, but like Cincinnati, only for one night when the letters suggested they stayed there at least a week. Another hotel called the Circle Park had the entry of Mrs. Georgia Howard, and Geyer recognized another common alias and speculated it was Georgia Yoke. The proprietor recognized the couple in the photograph, but they had no children with them. The couple stayed four days and Yoke and the owner of the hotel had a few conversations where Yoke spoke of her wealthy husband and his various business and real estate ventures. After chasing down the proprietor of a closed business, the detectives found the children were staying in another hotel. The proprietor there said that the children were homesick and crying often. The boy was getting into trouble which angered Holmes.

Geyer went to Chicago next where police offered no help nor seemed to have any knowledge of Holmes. He then went to Detroit, the last lead from Alice's letters. By following the same kinds of trails through the hotels, Geyer found that now Holmes had added Carrie and her other two children to another hotel in the city and was now shuffling around three parties in his menagerie. He was, strangely, keeping Alice, Nellie and Howard separate from their mother. Geyer suddenly realized that this was a game of possession for Holmes. One thing troubled him further, in the last letter written by Alice it is clear that Howard was no longer with them.

Meanwhile Holmes sat in prison in Philadelphia and read news stories about his increasing notoriety. It was reported that Geyer was hunting for the missing children. He also worked on writing his memoir, which the author maintains is a clear attempt to paint himself as a highly cultivated and disciplined man. In a letter to Carrie Pitezel he wrote from prison, he again insisted the children were in London with Miss W. Meanwhile he was no doubt pleased to speculate that Geyer would soon give up his hunt.

In early July, based on what lead is unclear, Detective Geyer and a new assistant detective Alf Cuddy found another similar pattern in Toronto. A young boy was not among the party. A tip came in from Thomas Ryves who had seen the description of Holmes in the paper, and recognized him as someone that rented the neighboring house in October of

1894. Meanwhile Geyer had become a national sensation given the horror that a man may have killed three children inflicted upon the nation in those days. The romanticism of this lone man traveling all over in search of the children captured the hearts and imaginations of many.

Thomas Ryves remembered the tenant because of his odd behavior. He came with little furniture, mainly a mattress and a huge trunk. He asked to borrow a shovel to dig a cellar for potatoes, then gave the shovel back and left forever with the trunk. Upon inspecting the cellar of the house, the detectives found evidence of bodies and called the coroner. The desiccated bodies of Alice and Nellie were removed by the coroner. Nellie's feet were amputated by the murderer to keep her club foot from offering information about her identity. The coroner surmised that the girls had been locked into the trunk and then killed with gas, evidenced by a hole drilled in the side of the trunk.

Holmes read the papers the next morning. In his memoir he blamed Minnie Williams, suggesting that she had a mysterious associate that did her bidding and was sure to be the one that killed the children. He maintained this story later that day when summoned to the District Attorney's office. Holmes focused on completing his memoir as he wanted to influence public opinion about him before the trial. He found a journalist willing to help him by the name of John King.

When the girls bodies were found, it caused the Chicago Police to inspect the building in Englewood. It soon became clear that Holmes was a monster beyond reckoning. The architecture in the top two floors struck them first. The many strange rooms, some airtight with gas lines controlled from Holmes's office confounded police. However, the worse revelations came in the basement. There they found human rib and skull bones in a vat of acid, piles quicklime, the coffin sized kiln, and a collection of surgical tools. They found many other remains as well: more bones, bloodstained clothes, vaults buried in the ground containing human remains, and a chain found in the ashes of a stove speculated to be a gift to Minnie. Charles Chappell came forward and helped detectives find another hidden chamber as well as information to find the articulated skeletons. Inside the door of the vault adjacent to the office they found the footprint etched into enamel that they believed to be that of Emeline Cigrand.

At first, when the remains of a child were found at the basement in Englewood, Geyer thought they might be the remains of Howard who he still sought. However, the coroner ruled that out since the bones were that of a little girl, likely Pearl Conner. He continued his search. On the night of August 18, the dark castle on Sixty-third and Wallace burned down, likely arson. Following a gut feeling, Geyer and his new assistant W. E Gary pursued hundreds of leads in Indianapolis, when finally they found a small real estate office in Irvington where a man remembered being pressured to give up the keys to a home for rent by Holmes. They found that Holmes had had a large woodstove installed in the house. The investigation found teeth and a fragment of jaw as well as some organs that had been packed too tightly to burn in the ashes. In addition, items such as Howard's coat, scarf pin and a small tin toy that his father had bought for him at the World's Fair, were found at the scene allowing for identification.

A Philadelphia grand jury indicted Holmes for murder in the case of Benjamin Pitezel. Indianapolis did the same for the murder of Howard Pitezel. Holmes was indicted in Toronto for the murders of Alice and Nellie. Newspapers continued to be baffled that the Chicago police had done nothing during Holmes's murderous spree in Chicago.

EPILOGUE: THE LAST CROSSING

The impact of the World's Columbian Exhibition on the psyche of America, argues Larson, has been profound. Many artists, architects, engineers and others who have shaped America in the years since were deeply impacted by visiting the fair. The Magic Kingdom of Walt Disney may have been influenced by the fact that his father was among the workers who built the White City. L. Frank Baum and William Wallace Denslow, creators of the Wizard of Oz both visited the fair. More significantly, however, the nation has been impacted in a broader way by setting in the imagination of a generation that a city need not be a filthy place, but can be a place of beauty. The neoclassical design showcased at the fair has impacted American architecture in many ways since, including the Lincoln Memorial.

In the years after the fair, Burnham was consulted by many cities on how to better plan their urban areas to reflect a higher aesthetic. He did this consulting work for free and impacted the designs of places such as Cleveland, Manila, San Francisco, and Washington D.C. He also offered ideas to Chicago, many of which were used, including the lakefront parks and Soldier Field.

Others have been critical of the turn towards what many think of as the obsoleteness of the neoclassical style. Among the earliest and most vocal was Louis Sullivan. His life after the fair took a turn for the worse. Having an intolerable attitude did not help him gain colleagues or clients and he sank into alcoholism and bromide use. He continued to design buildings, but at a rate of about one annually. His memoir was very critical of the effects of the fair in terms of reigniting a passion for neoclassical architecture, claiming that it stymied what would have otherwise been a period of incredible creative growth for American architecture. Frank Lloyd Wright would later take up the same cause. The academic tide shifted in architecture and Sullivan's views became predominant in the discipline.

Burnham's personal success and sense of accomplishment, however, would not be marred by these changes. His own career went on to be very successful. He was early on the environmentalist movement in architecture and city planning. In his fifties his health declined with the onset of colitis and diabetes.

Olmsted's health never improved and his memory was on the decline by 1895. His mental conditioned worsened into paranoia and at times violent outbursts. He was eventually sent to the McLean Asylum, a place that he had himself designed the grounds for, although he was plagued by the same kinds of modifications to his work that had troubled him with his other landscaping designs. He died August 28, 1903.

Ferris was forced to sell most of his ownership in the wheel due to the effects of the depression on the steel inspection business, and the lack of novelty of the ride, moved to the North Side of Chicago after the fair. He died of typhoid in November of 1896 at the age of thirty-seven.

Prendergast was tried in December of 1893. The prosecuting attorney was Alfred S. Trude. His defense argued for his insanity, but the jury was not convinced. He continued to write Trude cards throughout the trial. He was sentenced to death and executed.

The judge in the case of Herman W. Mudgett, alias H. H. Holmes, denied the prosecution the opportunity to bring forth witnesses not directly related to the Pitezel murder, leaving a great hole in the historical record as to what we know about Holmes. When Mrs. Pitezel was on the stand she was asked to identify the handwriting in the letters from her children that were never mailed, and it was clear she had not until that moment known of their existence. Reporters noted that Holmes expressed no emotions. He was found guilty and sentenced to hang.

While awaiting trial, Holmes wrote a confession admitting to murdering twenty-seven people, although some later turned out to still be alive. He also claimed to be physically transforming into the devil incarnate. The exact number of people he killed is unknown, although nine victims are known: Pearl and Julia Conner, Emeline Cigrand, the Williams sisters, and Ben, Alice, Nellie and Howard Pitezel. He was executed on May 7, 1896. Ironically, Holmes had a fear of having his body tampered with after his death. He provided strict instructions for the burial of his body that included cementing his unembalmed body in cement, then sinking the cement filled coffin into a double grave also filled with cement.

Strange deaths followed his execution. The foreman of the jury died of electrocution. Detective Geyer soon became very seriously sick. The warden killed himself. The priest the delivered last rights was found mysteriously dead. The office of the D.A. in Holmes's case burned to the ground and a single photograph of Holmes remained untouched.

In the final passage the author returns to the opening vignette where Burnham waits anxiously for news of Frank Millet aboard the *Olympic's* sister ship, the *Titanic*. His friend, however, was lost. He died forty-seven days later from a coma likely induced by a combination of his maladies, on June 1, 1912.

ANALYSIS

Erik Larson has produced another masterful work of historical non-fiction with *Devil in the White City*. A great strength of Larson's work in general, and this book is no exception, is the incredible amount of detail that he manages to cram into the pages of the book, all from firsthand primary research. Sources include letters, diaries, newspaper articles, archived documents, trial records and H. H. Holmes's confessions and memoirs. There are a few times where the narrative can devolve into mind numbingly long lists, particularly when ticking off the features of the fair itself. Likewise, the sheer size of the cast of characters that the author choses to explore sometimes interferes with the readability of the book. However, this level of detail is likely what many readers expect and appreciate about Larson's work so the effect is subjective.

The book has copious quotes throughout the text that add to the credibility and richness of the narrative overall. However, the quotes do not have direct links to the reference section which would have added value to the book. Instead, the reader is left wondering as to the context of the quotes in several cases. Instead of providing links in text, the author has chosen a style of referencing where there is simply a list of abbreviated references in the "Notes and Sources Section" which requires jumping back and forth to the back of the volume, and is cumbersome. It takes away from the overall experience of the book. Likewise, the lack of images included in this long volume is disappointing.

The overall thematic message of the dueling binaries of creation and destruction are clear and consistent throughout the book. The genesis of the White City lives in a dialectical tension with the palatable decay and vice ridden streets of the second largest American city at the turn of the century. Burnham is the clear hero of the narrative, positioned as the triumphant creator of a fair completely successful in its ability to conjure a momentary vision of urban splendor so compelling that it pierced the material realities of a Chicago where the bodies of animals rotted in the streets, organized crime corrupted even the highest officials, and the contaminated water supply routinely spread disease.

H. H. Holmes is, however, given a more nuanced treatment from the author. The style and efficiency of his methods seem clearly inspired by the industrialized killing of the slaughterhouses, a parallel alluded to often. At the same time, Holmes is representative of a confounding new reality not yet understood enough to be recognized by both police and the many people who simply could perceive the evil right in front of them. Readers today will be confronted with the cultural shift that has occurred in the last century when they read with disbelief the amount of what would now be clear evidence of suspicious behavior that went unnoticed by people at the turn of the century.

At times the author over extends into speculation on the motivations and inner logic of Holmes without a clear evidence trail to support those conclusions. Another disappointment concerning the coverage of Holmes's activities lies not with the author, but the scarcity of information available, due in part to the destruction of evidence prior to the completion of the Chicago investigation, and the lack of prosecuting evidence allowed at his trial concerning other crimes. The reader is left with more questions than answers concerning the breadth of his murderous acts.

What does come across very clearly is a sense for the cultural sensibilities of the day, and a lens of viewing history through which even seemingly disconnected events have deep symbolic connections. Larson manages to do this without leaving the impression that these associations are contrived. Despite the stark contrast of the White City and Holmes's castle of murder, the reader never loses sight of the fact that these fantasies and nightmares are both evoked from the same dream. In this way the book is relevant not just as an historical lesson, but an opportunity to reflect on the continuation of these dichotomies and how they persist side by side in today's America.

Made in the USA
Coppell, TX
01 June 2020

26796973R00066